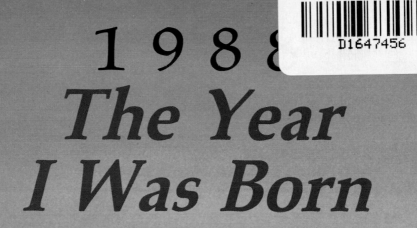

1988
The Year
I Was Born

Compiled by Sally Tagholm

Illustrated by Michael Evans

FANTAIL

in association with Signpost Books

FANTAIL
Published by the Penguin Group
Penguin Books Ltd, 27 Wrights Lane, London W8 5TZ, England
Penguin Books USA Inc., 375 Hudson Street, New York, NY 10014, USA
Penguin Books Australia Ltd., Ringwood, Victoria, Australia
Penguin Books Canada Ltd, 10 Alcorn Avenue, Toronto, Ontario,
Canada L3R 1B4
Penguin Books (NZ) Ltd., 182–190 Wairau Road, Auckland 10, New Zealand,

Published by Penguin Books in association with Signpost Books

First published 1993
10 9 8 7 6 5 4 3 2 1

Based on an original idea by Sally Wood
Conceived, designed and produced by Signpost Books Ltd, 1993
Copyright in this format © 1993 Signpost Books Ltd.,
25 Eden Drive, Headington, Oxford OX3 0AB, England

Illustrations copyright © 1993 Michael Evans
Text copyright © 1993 Sally Tagholm

Editor: Dorothy Wood
Art Director: Treld Bicknell
Paste up: Naomi Games

ISBN 1 874785 09 0 Hardback edition
ISBN 0140 90115 9 Paperback edition

Acknowledgements
The Olympic Symbol on pp. 16 and 37 is reproduced with the consent of the
International Olympic Committee.

Colour separations by Fotographics, Ltd.
Printed and bound in Belgium by Proost Book Production through
Landmark Production Consultants, Ltd.

Typeset by DP Photosetting, Aylesbury, Bucks

MY FAMILY

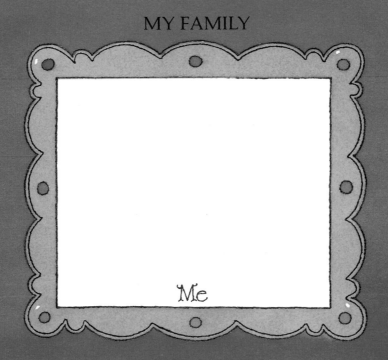

Me

Name:
Date of birth:
Time of birth:
Place of birth:
Weight at birth:
Colour of eyes:
Colour of hair (if any):
Distinguishing marks:

Mum

Dad

Sister/Brother

Sister/Brother

January

Friday *January 1*	Bank Holiday. A train of 10 camels arrives in Adelaide, South Australia, after a 117 day trans-continental expedition from Darwin to celebrate Australia's 200th birthday.
Saturday *January 2*	Watch out for a plague of Red Pharaoh ants in Hammersmith and Fulham, London. The first Little Bustard to visit Britain for 12yrs is spotted in Burton, Dorset. It's a large, long-legged game bird that breeds in southern Europe, Asia and Africa.
Sunday *January 3*	Woolly Rhino Torgamba's sleeping quarters at Port Lympne Zoo, nr Hythe, Kent, are badly damaged by high winds and keepers use portable gas heaters to keep her warm.
Monday *January 4*	17 holidaymakers are rescued by a passing ship after being stranded on Lundy Island in the Bristol Channel for 5 days.
Tuesday *January 5*	Comic Relief is launched in London by Rowan Atkinson. Red noses cost 50p each. 50 cashmere goats from New Zealand are put into quarantine at Heathrow after eating their own import documents.
Wednesday *January 6*	Christmas Day or Old Yule is celebrated on the Island of Fula in the Shetlands. The 50 people who live there still use the old Julian calendar.
Thursday *January 7*	A golden retriever called Prince (4) convalesces at home in Warrington, Cheshire, after being fitted with a heart pacemaker at Liverpool University Small Animal's Hospital.
Friday *January 8*	An earthquake in Potenza, Southern Italy, measures 4.2 on the Richter Scale. At least 60 people die when a huge snowstorm covers most of the eastern United States.
Saturday *January 9*	The Lord Mayor of London and the Lady Mayoress, Sir Greville and Lady Spratt, hold a Fancy Dress party for 600 children at the Mansion House.
Sunday *January 10*	The third annual Husky Sled Dog Rally is held in Sherwood Forest, Notts. The fastest time over a 7.56km course is 17min 32.16secs.
Monday *January 11*	Florence Knapp (114) dies in Philadelphia, USA. *The Guinness Book of Records* says she was the oldest person in the world.
Tuesday *January 12*	Private view of new life-sized robotic dinosaurs at the Natural History Museum in London: they include a duck-billed Corythosaurus, a bird-like Gallimimus and a large lizard-like creature called a Scolosaurus.

January

Named after the Roman god Janus who had two faces and could look backwards and forwards at the same time; also known as 'frosty month', 'after-yule', 'first-month' and 'snow-month'.

Happy Birthday Australia!

It is exactly 200 years since settlers from Britain first arrived in Australia. Ten camels launch a special year of celebrations and parties when they arrive in Adelaide at one minute past midnight on January 1 at the end of the Trans-Australia Camel Trek. They set off from Darwin, on the north coast, on September 6, 1987 and travelled 3,426km across the heart of Australia, following the route of the first telegraph line, which was built in 1872. It took the camels 117 days at an average speed of 40km a day. The trek was partly organised by the South Australian Police, which was the first police force in the world to use camels for patrol work.

AUSTRALIA FACT FILE '88

Population: 16,538,200
Area: 7,682,000sq. km
Prime Minister: Bob Hawke
Capital: Canberra

The Aborigines, who lived in Australia for hundreds of years before the British arrived, declare 1988 a Year of Mourning. They throw wreaths into Botany Bay, where Capt. James Cook first landed in 1770.

Camels played a vital part in exploring and developing the heart of Australia—carrying people and heavy loads over huge distances. The original railway line, from Adelaide to Alice Springs, was called 'The Ghan', after the Afghan camel drivers, who helped to make it possible.

The Bugle ▲
EEC BANS CHEAP CHINESE KNICKERS IN BRITAIN

Daily Chuckle
DINOSAUR FOOTPRINTS GIVEN STATE PROTECTION IN SOVIET CENTRAL ASIA

Blurb ☆
1,000 RED TELEPHONE BOXES TO BE SAVED

World
INFLAMMABLE FOAM FURNITURE TO BE BANNED

Wednesday *January 13*	The first edition of a new children's newspaper called *Early Times* goes on sale today—price 50p.
Thursday *January 14*	Lieut. Rupert Novis, of the Coldstream Guards, is presented with a Royal Humane Society silver medal for saving a boy (13) from the jaws of a 3.35m crocodile in the river Zambesi, Zimbabwe.
Friday *January 15*	The biggest purpose-built cruise ship in the world, the *Sovereign of the Seas*, is named in Miami today. She weighs 75,184 tonnes and carries 2,276 passengers.
Saturday *January 16*	Start of the Monte Carlo Rally. A rare lesser white-fronted goose from Siberia arrives at the Wildfowl Trust, Slimbridge, Gloucs. Twitchers flock to see it.
Sunday *January 17*	The pond surrounding the Old Jewel House, opposite the House of Lords, is cleaned out. It's full of coins thrown in by visitors to London. They are donated to the RNLI.
Monday *January 18*	9 square-rigged ships, which left Portsmouth last year to re-enact the First Fleet's voyage to Australia 200yrs ago, sail into Botany Bay. Sir Thomas Sopwith, the famous aviator, is 100 today.
Tuesday *January 19*	The Post Office issues 4 new stamps to celebrate the 200th birthday of the Linnean Society. Carl Linnaeus was a Swedish naturalist who invented the system of names for species of plants and animals that we use today. His collection included 19,000 pages of pressed flowers. New Moon
Wednesday *January 20*	A huge 464yr-old cannon, which belonged to Suleiman the Magnificent, is displayed outside the British Museum, London. The barrel has 16 sides and is almost 4.88m long.
Thursday *January 21*	Brian Milton, who took off from London's City Airport on December 2 in his microlight 'Dalgety Flyer', lands in Darwin, North Australia. His 36-day journey breaks the record—although his plane can only carry fuel for 9hrs and has a maximum speed of 152.88kph.
Friday *January 22*	Heavy snow falls in Wales, the West of England, the North and the Midlands. Blizzards close East Midlands and Manchester Airports. 100 schools are closed in Shropshire.
Saturday *January 23*	Japan's newest magnetic levitation train, the Maglev, reaches 257.48kph in 30secs during tests in Miyazaki.

Sunday
January 24

20 firemen are called to Dungeness Nuclear Power Plant in Kent after 2.03 tonnes of radioactive gas escapes.

Monday
January 25

Britain's official 200th birthday present to Australia is a 203.20 tonne brigantine called *Young Endeavour*, named after Captain Cook's ship.

Heavy rain all over Britain

Tuesday
January 26

Australia Day: hundreds of small boats greet the procession of 160 tall ships re-enacting the anchoring of the First Fleet ships 200yrs ago in Sydney Harbour. It's the 300th anniversary of the Great Fire of Bungay, Suffolk, in 1688.

Wednesday
January 27

Work starts on Scarborough Pier in Yorkshire to get rid of the gribble—a kind of underwater death watch beetle which has been eating away at the timber.

Thursday
January 28

The Pink Floyd pop group launches its first tour in Britain for 7yrs with an inflatable bed floating over the River Thames in London. 30,000 pink balloons are released all over the country.

Friday
January 29

1.52m floods in Kent and Essex. Cars float down the A414 at Maldon, Essex. The Thames Water Authority issues its first red alert for almost 10yrs as the river threatens to burst its banks at Sunbury, Teddington and Staines.

Saturday
January 30

5 NATO mine sweepers visit the Pool of London and are open to the public.

Sunday
January 31

The wettest January since records began, with more than 10.16cm falling in Central London. The red alert on the Thames continues for the third day.

January 19: PO issues 4 stamps to commemorate the 200th birthday of the Linnean Society

18p

Bull-rout *Myoxocephalus scorpius*
THE LINNEAN SOCIETY 1788/1988

26p

Yellow Waterlily *Nuphar lutea*
THE LINNEAN SOCIETY 1788/1988

31p

Bewick's Swan *Cygnus columbianus*
THE LINNEAN SOCIETY 1788/1988

34p

Morel *Morchella esculenta*
THE LINNEAN SOCIETY 1788/1988

February

Monday
February 1

Tony Mann, from Chulmleigh, Devon, wins the Toymaker of the Year award at the British Toymakers' Guild Show and 'Sylvanian Family' is named Best Toy of the Year.

Tuesday
February 2

'The Gold of the Pharaohs' exhibition opens in Edinburgh. A gold mask of the Pharaoh Psusennes is valued at more than £20,000,000.

Full Moon

Wednesday
February 3

A replica of the ship of the Portuguese explorer Bartolomeu Dias, the first European to round the Cape of Good Hope, South Africa, in 1488, lands at Mossel Bay, Cape Province, re-enacting the original 88-day journey from Lisbon.

Thursday
February 4

Suffragette Mrs Catherine Griffiths (102), goes back to the House of Commons to celebrate the 70th anniversary of the granting of votes for women. She was imprisoned for trying to put nails on the Prime Minister's seat.

Friday
February 5

The first Comic Relief Red Nose Day raises £7,000,000 for starving people in Africa.

Saturday
February 6

Radio Laser, the 3yr-old pirate station, goes off air when her ship *Communicator* slips anchor off the Essex coast.

Sunday
February 7

More than 50 clowns pay tribute to Joseph Grimaldi at the Annual Clowns' Service at Holy Trinity Church, Dalston, London.

Monday
February 8

Michael Jackson, U2, George Michael, Alison Moyet and the Pet Shop Boys win awards at the British Record Industry Awards Ceremony at the Royal Albert Hall, London.

Tuesday
February 9

A famous mountain dog, a border collie called Loch, disappears in a blizzard after taking part in a rescue on Helvellyn in the Lake District. Four Romans are reburied in the graveyard of St Andrew's Church, Scole, Norfolk, 1600yrs after they died. Their remains were discovered 3yrs ago.

Wednesday
February 10

A National Amphibian Survey is launched to count frogs, toads and newts. Particularly at risk is the great crested newt and the common toad.

Thursday
February 11

The 92nd Cruft's Dog Show opens at Earls Court, London: altogether 15,557 dogs enter in 1949 classes.

Earthquake in Los Angeles measures 5 on the Richter Scale

February

The Roman month of purification. It has also been known as 'sprout kale', 'rain-month', 'month of cakes' and 'month of ravaging wolves'.

The Winter Olympics
(February 13–28)

The first Winter Olympics were held in 1924 in Chamonix, France. Since then, they have been held all over the world—in Switzerland, USA, Germany, Norway, Italy, Austria, Japan, Yugoslavia and this year, for the first time, in Canada. The host city is Calgary—often known as 'Cow City'. There are 1700 competitors from 58 different countries, including Eddie 'The Eagle' Edwards, from Cheltenham, Britain's only ski-jumper at this year's Winter Olympics. He wears a helmet with EAGLE written on it in gold felt-tip pen, and has problems with his thick glasses steaming up. Lots of things seem to go wrong for Eddie, and he ends up borrowing a pair of skis from the Australians, a ski suit from the West Germans, and goggles from the Italians. With only 2yrs experience, he comes last in both his events (70m and 90m) but still manages to beat the British record with a jump of 71m.

The official Olympic souvenir is a bear called Howdy, who wears a white cowboy hat and a waistcoat embroidered with the five Olympic rings and a snowflake, which is the logo for this year's Games.

Chinese Year of the Dragon

According to legend, the Buddha summoned all the animals in the world to him one New Year, and promised them all a reward. Only twelve obeyed and he gave them each a year: the Rat arrived first so he got the first year! The order of the 12-year cycle is always the same: Rat, Buffalo, Tiger, Rabbit, Dragon, Snake, Horse, Goat, Monkey, Cockerel, Dog and Pig.

Dragons are usually healthy, enthusiastic and energetic but they lose their tempers rather easily and can be a bit stubborn. They are very self-sufficient and often enjoy being alone. They are generous and intelligent—perfectionists who ask a lot of other people and of themselves. People born under this sign should go far and will shine in whatever they choose to do.

Dragons get on well with Rats, Snakes, Cockerels and Monkeys but NOT with Tigers or Dogs. Famous Dragons include Joan of Arc, Sigmund Freud, Sarah Bernhardt, Salvador Dali, Napoleon III and Jesus Christ.

The Year of the Rabbit finishes on Feb. 17. Rabbits are usually very happy and land on their feet. They are very sociable and love parties! Famous Rabbits include Queen Victoria and Albert Einstein.

Friday *February 12*	The Queen visits the Wildfowl Trust, Slimbridge, Gloucs, and opens a new hide for watching wild swans. A rare Georgian wooden doll in her original silk dress and linen petticoat is sold for £7,000 at Bonham's, London.
Saturday *February 13*	At 1am the two biggest planets, Saturn and Uranus, are in conjunction—which means that they are in a straight line with Earth. This only happens twice in a century. The opening ceremony for the 15th Winter Olympics takes place at Calgary, Alberta, Canada.
Sunday *February 14*	Valentine's Day. A 3yr-old English Setter called Starlite Express of Valsett (known as Bonnie) wins the Supreme Champion title at Cruft's Dog Show.
Monday *February 15*	Eddie 'The Eagle' Edwards, from Cheltenham, comes last out of 58 competitors in the 70m ski-jump at the Winter Olympics.
Tuesday *February 16*	The Pancake Bell at Scarborough is rung at midday to start the Shrovetide Skipping Festival on the South Foreshore. It's so cold in the Arctic that polar bears can walk across the ice between Greenland and Iceland.
Wednesday *February 17*	Start of the Chinese year of the Dragon. British soldiers get a new uniform today. It has been specially treated to stop infra-red radiation that can be picked up by enemy sensors. The new clip-on bayonet comes complete with bottle-opener. New Moon
Thursday *February 18*	A lock of Admiral Nelson's grey-blond hair is sold for £5,000 at auction in Crewkerne, Somerset. It is at least 183yrs old.
Friday *February 19*	Mr Gerry Blood is appointed official artist of this year's Olympic Games by the International Olympic Committee.
Saturday *February 20*	Twin Golden Lion Tamarins called Martina and Geeles are born at Noorder Dierenpark Zoo, Holland. They are bright red dwarf monkeys from Brazil that are almost extinct.
Sunday *February 21*	Worcester Cathedral launches a £10,000,000 appeal for repairs to its 14th century tower. A large nylon safety net is put up to protect the choir and congregation from falling stone.
Monday *February 22*	Ganesh Sittipalam (8), from Surbiton, passes Maths 'O' level with a Grade A. Archaeologists find the grave of Boadicea, the warrior Queen, under platform 8 at King's Cross Station, London.

| **Tuesday February 23** | Prince Charles announces that he has banned aerosols from his household. Scaffolding goes up around the Sphinx of Giza, nr Cairo, Egypt, after a large limestone lump falls off her right shoulder. |

Tuesday February 23

Prince Charles announces that he has banned aerosols from his household. Scaffolding goes up around the Sphinx of Giza, nr Cairo, Egypt, after a large limestone lump falls off her right shoulder.

Wednesday February 24

An RAF Phantom jet flies from Land's End to John O'Groats at an average speed of 1,223kph and sets a new record time of 46mins, 44secs. The Queen comes top of *Money Magazine*'s survey of the richest people in Britain with £3,340,000,000.

Thursday February 25

The Manchester Championship Dog Show opens at the G-Mex Centre: there are more than 10,000 entries.

Friday February 26

6000 swimmers take part in Swimathon '88, a 3-day swimming marathon at the Queen Mother Sports Centre, Victoria, to raise £500,000 for Great Ormond Street Children's Hospital.

Great Ormond Street Hospital Marathon

Saturday February 27

A team from the Museum of London finds the remains of a Roman amphitheatre underneath Guildhall in the City of London. The arena where gladiators used to fight lies under Guildhall Yard.

Sunday February 28

Official closing ceremony of the Winter Olympics in Calgary, with the Soviet Union topping the medals table with 11 gold, 9 silver and 9 bronze.

Monday February 29

Leap Year's Day and Superman's 50th birthday. Emma Birch of Newcastle-under-Lyme, Staffs is 100 today—although it's only the 25th time she's actually celebrated her birthday.

It's been the sunniest February in London since records began in 1929

The British Family 1988

Mr and Mrs 1988 and the little 1988s spend, on average, £10.33 each on food a week. They each drink 4.01 pints of milk and cream and eat 117.08g of cheese, 1.03kg of meat, 143g of fish, 2.67 eggs, 279.53g of fat and oil, 249.19g of sugar and preserves, 3.25kg of fresh fruit and vegetables, 127.18g of bread and cereals and 75.41g of beverages.

Milk and cream	112.46p
Cheese	38.21p
Meat	303.65p
Fish	57.63p
Eggs	19.32p
Fats and oil	34.51p
Sugar and preserves	17.77p
Fruit and vegetables	226.99p
Bread and cereals	180.17p
Beverages	42.34p
	1033.05p = £10.33

March

**Tuesday
March 1**

St David's Day. Chocolate rationing (198.44gms a month per child) is abolished in Poland.

**Wednesday
March 2**

The Soviet credit card is launched today. Thousands of dead fish, mostly roach and bream, are found at Potter Heigham, Norfolk, after gales sweep sea water into the Norfolk Broads.

**Thursday
March 3**

More than 2,000 people welcome ski-jumper Eddie 'The Eagle' Edwards home to Cheltenham after the Winter Olympics. New Social and Liberal Democratic party (SLD) is born.

Full Moon

Gales sweep Scotland; 111kph gust recorded on Forth Road Bridge

**Friday
March 4**

A new version of the Welsh Bible (*Y Beibl Cymraeg*) is published. The first one was translated in 1588. Large cracks are found in Edward III's Round Tower at Windsor Castle.

**Saturday
March 5**

The 1988 Iditarod Trail, a 1609.3km dog sled race between Anchorage and Nome, starts in Alaska.

**Sunday
March 6**

Start of European Year of the Environment's Woodlands and Forests Week. A 508-tonne West German submarine crashes into a Norwegian oil rig in the North Sea.

**Monday
March 7**

Queen Elizabeth's Pocket Pistol, a 10.16 tonne bronze gun that is more than 400yrs old, is moved into Dover Castle to protect it from the weather.

**Tuesday
March 8**

International Women's Day. A 1907 Rolls Royce Silver Ghost is flown from Manchester to Tokyo for the opening of their first Japanese showroom. It is silver-plated and worth over £5,000,000.

**Wednesday
March 9**

National No Smoking Day. An 18th-century teapot in the shape of a sumo wrestler fetches £36,300 at Phillips auction rooms in London.

**Thursday
March 10**

A square wooden plate salvaged from the wreck of HMS *Invincible*, which sank off Portsmouth in 1758, is sold for £1,045 at Christies, London. Two hand grenades fetch £990.

**Friday
March 11**

Sir Ranulph Fiennes, Oliver Shepard and Dr Mike Stroud set off from Ward Hunt Island to walk across the frozen Arctic Ocean to the North Pole, with no dogs, motor vehicles or help from aircraft.

**Saturday
March 12**

Goodbye to the English pound note at midnight tonight, first introduced exactly 191yrs ago. 160 crews take part in the Yorkshire Head of the River Race—4.83km along the River Ouse.

March

Named after Mars, the Roman God of War. It has also been known as 'rough-month', 'lengthening-month', 'boisterous-month' and 'windy-month'.

HMS *Invincible*

The first HMS *Invincible* was a French warship captured by the English in 1747. She sank in 1758, when she hit a sand-bank off St Helens, Isle of Wight.

More than 220 years later, in 1979, a huge salvage operation was mounted, and a hoard of interesting objects was brought up from the wreck. Lots of them are sold this year, including leather shoes, a woollen sock, a ball of wool, ropes, cannon wheels and sand-glasses—as well as hand grenades and a square wooden plate (see March 10).

The sand-glasses (28secs and 14secs) were used for timing the ship's watch and for measuring speed. Knots were tied on the Log line and the ship's speed was calculated from the number of knots run out while the sand-glass emptied. The sailor's square wooden plate was the origin of the phrase 'a square meal'.

March 1:
PO issues 4 new stamps to mark the 400th anniversary of the Welsh bible

March 22:
PO issues 4 new stamps celebrating gymnastics, skiing, tennis and football

Crescendo ▲
EXPEDITION SETS OFF FROM LONDON ZOO IN SEARCH OF THE ST. HELENA GIANT EARWIG

Blabber Mouth ◉
PEACE CAMPAIGNERS CLIMB NELSON'S COLUMN TO PROTEST ABOUT ACID RAIN

Daily Whoop ☆
UNDERGROUND PASSENGERS HIJACK TUBE TRAIN IN PROTEST AT POOR SERVICE

Hedgehog
ROYAL SKI PARTY IN AVALANCHE TRAGEDY

Sunday *March 13*	Mothering Sunday. Jon Sanders lands at Fremantle, Australia, after sailing non-stop 3 times round the world on his own. It took him 658 days in his 14m sloop *Parry Endeavour*. **Avalanches in Austria**
Monday *March 14*	Commonwealth Day. Developers re-route a new road in West Thurrock, Essex, to save a rare species of tiny spider, Zodarion italicum, which lives in an old quarry there.
Tuesday *March 15*	Budget Day: the standard rate of income tax is cut by 2p to 25p in the pound. A public inquiry opens into a scheme to mine cat litter (fuller's earth) at Bletchingley, Surrey.
Wednesday *March 16*	British scientists from the Natural History Museum and Kingston Polytechnic report a new species of dinosaur found in the Sahara desert: a huge, herbivorous Sauropod up to 20m long.
Thursday *March 17*	St Patrick's Day: the Queen Mother presents shamrock to the Irish Guards at Chelsea Barracks. Alexandra Palace in north London is re-opened after being destroyed by fire in 1980.
Friday *March 18*	The Queen opens the new £250,000,000 North Terminal at Gatwick Airport. The European Space Agency and NASA agree to build the first international space station. It will go into orbit in the late 1990s. New Moon
Saturday *March 19*	The Pilgrims Way Centre opens in Canterbury. Swarms of desert locusts are spotted on the border of Tunisia and Libya in N. Africa.
Sunday *March 20*	51st veteran motorcycle run from Epsom, Surrey, to Brighton. An Alpine swift, which was blown off course from the Mediterranean, is flown from Birmingham Airport to Faro in Portugal on a scheduled BA flight.
Monday *March 21*	Spring Equinox. The Wall's Ice Cream Pocket Money Monitor shows that average weekly pocket money has risen by 6% in the last year—to £1.23p.
Tuesday *March 22*	European Environment Year ends today. Mrs Thatcher, the Prime Minister, spends 15mins picking up banana skins, crisp packets and other rubbish in St James's Park, London, at the beginning of her Clean Nineties campaign.
Wednesday *March 23*	The 36th Regiment, Royal Engineers rebuild the gravel islands where common terns breed at Dungeness, Kent, before the birds arrive back from Africa. The islands were badly damaged by the hurricane last October.

Thursday *March 24*	The Soviet Union launches a spacecraft to carry supplies to two cosmonauts on the space station *Mir* where they have been in orbit since last December. A 132.96kph gust of wind recorded at Mallin Head, Ulster
Friday *March 25*	Sir Ranulph Fiennes and his team give up their expedition to the North Pole because of frost-bite. They have only covered 64.37km.
Saturday *March 26*	A major archaeological discovery of Bronze Age axe heads, swords and tools in north Norfolk is kept Top Secret to protect it from treasure hunters.
Sunday *March 27*	Start of British Summertime: clocks go forward one hour at 1am. Sir Ranulph Fiennes and his team are lifted off by a twin-engined otter plane and flown back to base camp on Ward Hunt Island.
Monday *March 28*	3000 balloons are launched at the Albert Docks, Liverpool, at the start of a new 'Discover Merseyside '88' campaign.
Tuesday *March 29*	A cow called Daisy is winched to safety by firemen after falling into a swamp near Colchester. Royal Navy bomb disposal experts detonate a 907.2kg World War II German torpedo after it gets caught in fishermen's nets 8.04km off the coast of Northumbria.
Wednesday *March 30*	Ian Botham and 3 elephants leave Perpignan to retrace Hannibal's journey through France and across the Alps to Italy. The elephants wear special boots to protect their feet on the hard roads.
Thursday *March 31*	Maundy Thursday. The traditional Maundy Service is held at Lichfield Cathedral, Staffs. The Queen presents special Maundy money to 124 pensioners—a man and a woman for each of her 62 years.

Happy Birthday

AUSTRALIA

Dublin is 1000 years old
The Welsh Bible is 400 years old
Australia is 200 years old
The Royal Philharmonic Society is 175 years old
The National Gallery, London, is 150 years old
The British Amateur Gymnastics Association
  is 100 years old
The Lawn Tennis Association is 100 years old
The Football League is 100 years old
Votes for women are 70 years old
Mickey Mouse is 60 years old
Tintin is 60 years old
Dandy and *Beano* are 50 years old

The Readers Digest is 50 years old
Superman is 50 years old
The Prince of Wales is 40 years old
The World Health Organisation is 40 years old
Israel is 40 years old
The Cadbury's National Exhibition of
                    Children's Art is 40 years old
The Citroën 2CV is 40 years old
London parking meters are 30 years old
The London Planetarium is 30 years old

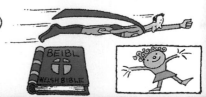

UK Fact File 1988

Leap Year   Olympic Year   MCMLXXXVIII

Total area of the United Kingdom   244,100sq kms

Capital City   London (1580sq kms)

Population of UK   57,065,000

Average population per sq km   234

Births      Marriages
787,600   394,000

Deaths 649,200

 Most popular   Most popular
girl's name*   boy's name*

Head of State   Queen Elizabeth II

Prime Minister
Margaret Hilda Thatcher

Astronomer Royal
Prof. Sir Francis Graham Smith

Poet Laureate
Edward (Ted) Hughes

Archbishop of Canterbury
Robert Alexander Kennedy Runcie

Royal Swan Keeper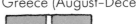
F.J. Turk

Members of Parliament   650 (523 for England, 38 for Wales, 72 for
Scotland and 17 for N. Ireland). 41 are
women

Presidency of EEC   Germany (Jan–July)   Greece (August–December)

Members of EEC   Belgium, Denmark, France, Federal Republic of Germany,
Greece, Ireland, Italy, Luxembourg, The Netherlands,
Portugal, Spain, the United Kingdom

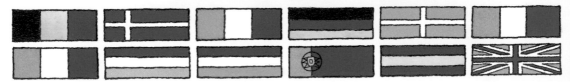

Highest temperature of the year 30.2°C at Cheltenham, Gloucs on
August 7

Lowest temperature of the year 　 –11.6°C at Carnwath, Strathclyde on
November 22

* according to *The Times* newspaper

April

The opening month—from the Latin 'Aperire', which means to open. Also known as the time of budding, the cuckoo's May or the fool's May.

Friday April 1
Good Friday. René Bricka sets off from Tenerife in the Canary Islands to walk across the Atlantic Ocean to the Caribbean on a pair of 4.57 metre polyester floats.

Saturday April 2
Oxford beats Cambridge by over 5 lengths to win the 134th Boat Race. A baby Lowland Gorilla called Asali (Swahili for Honey) is born at London Zoo. Full Moon

Sunday April 3
Easter Sunday. René Bricka (see April 1) has covered 72.42km of the Atlantic Ocean. He lives on vitamin pills and fish.

Monday April 4
Bank Holiday. Mark Ryder (26) eats 2000 baby eels in 20.5secs at Frampton on Severn, Gloucs., and wins the World Elver Eating title for the 6th year running.

Tuesday April 5
Work begins on a new £20,000,000 pipeline between an oil field in Poole Harbour, Dorset and the terminal on Southampton Water. It will carry 11,365,000 litres of crude oil a day.

Wednesday April 6
10,000th McDonald's hamburger restaurant opens in Dale City, Virginia, USA.

Thursday April 7
International No Smoking Day. Smoking is banned from all public places in New York; the King of Nepal orders all cigarette factories to shut for 2hrs, and there are 15p fines for lighting up in Peking.

Friday April 8
A new survey called Prodfact 1988 shows that we each eat more than 101.60kg of potatoes a year as well as 6.35kg of peas, 5.90kg of carrots, 56.70g of asparagus, 61.24kg of meat and drink 122.69 litres of milk.

Saturday April 9
National Daffodil Day. The 150th Grand National is won by 'Rhyme 'n' Reason', trained by David Elsworth and ridden by Brendan Powell. Heavy snow in Derbyshire

Sunday April 10
The 12.87km long Great Seto Bridge over the Inland Sea in Japan is officially opened. It carries both cars and trains and is the longest bridge of its kind in the world, connecting the smallest island, Shikoku, to the largest, Honshu.

Monday April 11	187 Australian Army Royal Guards are standing guard outside Buckingham Palace, Windsor Castle, St James's Palace and the Tower of London, as part of Australia's Bicentennial celebrations.
Tuesday April 12	Cosmonaut's Day in the Soviet Union to celebrate the first space flight round the Earth by Yuri Gagarin in 1961. The first American pizza is sold in Moscow at 1.25 roubles (£1.25) a slice.
Wednesday April 13	Mother Teresa of Calcutta (77), who won the Nobel Peace Prize for her work with poor people in India, visits the Prime Minister at 10 Downing St.
Thursday April 14	A new Southern Region train reaches 175kph near Winchester and breaks the record for the 230.13km journey from Waterloo to Weymouth with a time of 119mins.
Friday April 15	The Princess Royal launches a new 4572 tonne nuclear submarine HMS *Talent* at Barrow-in-Furness with a bottle of rum instead of champagne. More than 500 women enter the first-ever beauty contest in Moscow.
Saturday April 16	New Moon A memorial plaque is unveiled in Ealing's Broadway Centre to author Frank Richards (real name Charles Hamilton) who invented Billy Bunter and Greyfriars School. He was born in Ealing, in 1876. FRANK RICHARDS
Sunday April 17	22,000 runners take part in the 8th London Marathon. Nigel Canham wins the 5th Blackawton International Festival of Worm Charming in Devon. He lures 128 worms out of a 1.22m × 0.91m patch of earth in 15mins.
Monday April 18	First day of Ramadan. The Somerset Trust for Nature Conservation launches a campaign to raise £20,000 to save Yarty Moor Bog, nr Taunton. It's the home of rare plants like the asphodel, pimpernel and pale butterwort.
Tuesday April 19	Ian Botham and two elephants (the third retired on vet's advice) arrive in Turin at the end of their 804.65km walk across the Alps in aid of the Leukaemia Research Fund. It took them 21 days.
Wednesday April 20	The Prince of Wales opens the 'Armada 400' exhibition at the National Maritime Museum, Greenwich, to celebrate the 400th anniversary of the defeat of the Spanish Armada. ARMADA 400 OPEN
Thursday April 21	The Queen celebrates her 62nd birthday in Australia. 5,000 people sing 'Happy Birthday' to her at a garden party at Government House, Perth. Later, she makes a special broadcast to children in the outback on the School of the Air.

Friday **April 22**	The 50th Hawaiian Goose this season hatches at the Wildfowl Trust, Slimbridge, Gloucs. It's an endangered species that declined from 25,000 in Hawaii in the 18th century to less than 50 birds in the 1940s.
Saturday **April 23**	National Spring Clean Day. Greek cycling champion, Kanellos Kanellopoulos, crosses the Aegean Sea from Crete to Santorini (119.09km) in a special pedal plane called 'Daedalus' with a wing span of 34.14m. It takes him 3hrs, 54mins.
Sunday **April 24**	139 competitors set off on the 3,355.39km Great Australian Camel Race from Ayers Rock to Carrara on the Queensland coast.
Monday **April 25**	Beginning of Save the Children Week. Sentries guard Charlie and Rhys, two of the ravens at the Tower of London who are sitting on eggs in a large, specially-built, nesting box in the shadow of the White Tower.
Tuesday **April 26**	The Government launches a campaign to save the Wart Biter (a large grasshopper), the Natterjack Toad, the Lundy Cabbage, Drooping Saxifrage, the Trembling Sea Mat and more than 1,000 other endangered species.
Wednesday **April 27**	A California Condor chick starts to peck its way out of its egg at San Diego Zoo. Keepers play recorded vulture noises to encourage it. Only 27 California Condors exist—all in captivity.
Thursday **April 28**	Three lighthouse keepers leave Flat Holm Island at the mouth of the Severn for the last time. After 250yrs, the light has been automated and will be run from Nash Point, nr Porthcawl.
Friday **April 29**	Opening of the Glasgow Garden Festival: the centrepiece of Stoke-on-Trent's China Garden display is a teapot that is 3.35m high and 4.57m wide.
Saturday **April 30**	The Queen opens Expo '88 in Brisbane, Australia, the first World Fair to be held in the southern hemisphere this century. She meets Bluey, a red-haired robot who says 'G'day'.

The Reporter
ADDER WARNINGS IN GLOUCESTERSHIRE

Chit-Chat ★
8 HEADED DAFFODIL IS GROWN IN NOTTINGHAMSHIRE

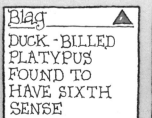

Blag ▲
DUCK-BILLED PLATYPUS FOUND TO HAVE SIXTH SENSE

Daily Scoop ◉
40-YEAR-OLD PUFF OF AIR FOUND IN NEW ZEALAND

May

Sunday *May 1*	Boots Over Scotland: more than 2,000 mountaineers try to climb every peak above 914.4m in Scotland. Full Moon
Monday *May 2*	Bank Holiday. The Art of Lego exhibition opens at Bodelwyddan Castle, Clwyd.
Tuesday *May 3*	Six huge Chinese dinosaur skeletons are dismantled after an exhibition in Cardiff. The bones are numbered and put into boxes, before being taken to the Natural History Museum, London.
Wednesday *May 4*	A 200yr-old pig sty near Ammanford, Dyfed, is made a listed building because of its 'architectural and historic interest'.
Thursday *May 5*	Children's Day in Japan—a national holiday. Climbers from China, Japan and Nepal take part in the first live TV broadcast from the top of Mount Everest. It commemorates the first conquest 35yrs ago by Sir Edmund Hillary and Tenzing Norgay.
Friday *May 6*	Worcestershire cricketer Graeme Hick scores 405 runs in a single innings at Taunton, Somerset. The Chancellor of the Exchequer, Nigel Lawson, attends the ceremony of the Trial of the Pyx, where new coins are tested. The new 5p and 10p pieces will be smaller and lighter, and will go into circulation in June 1990 and June 1992.
Saturday *May 7*	Helston Furry Dance in Cornwall celebrates the end of winter and beginning of summer.
Sunday *May 8*	A 48kg Indian Rhinoceros (Rhinoceros unicornis) called Ropen (which means Silver) is born at Whipsnade Park, Beds. Red sand blows in from the Sahara Desert and covers south and south west England.
Monday *May 9*	The only pair of breeding Golden Eagles in England hatch a chick in the Lake District. Prince Harry (3) has a hernia operation.
Tuesday *May 10*	The steam engine *Mallard*, which set a world speed record of 202.77kph in 1938, celebrates its 50th birthday by puffing down from the Railway Museum, York, to Marylebone, London.
Wednesday *May 11*	The Queen and the Duke of Edinburgh arrive back in England. While in Australia the Queen made 7 speeches, unveiled 16 plaques and a statue of herself, was given a new ceremonial carriage with electric windows and travelled 49,888km.
Thursday *May 12*	1988 Jersey Royal new potato season begins today. Stephen Venables, from Highbury, London, climbs Everest east face, which has never been climbed before without the use of oxygen

May

Takes its name from Maia, the goddess of growth and increase, or from 'maiores', the Latin word for elders, who were honoured this month. The Anglo Saxons called it 'thrimilce' because cows could be milked three times a day now. An old Dutch name was 'bloumaand' which means blossoming month.

MIGHTY'S GREAT JOURNEY

When Mighty, the Whitbread Shire horse, and Alison Payne set off from Hyde Park, London, on May 31, with a fanfare of trumpets from the Lifeguards, they were following in the hoofprints of a Great Journey made long ago, in 1698, by Celia Fiennes, the daughter of one of Cromwell's colonels. She travelled to every English county, often accompanied by only two servants, and wrote a brilliant journal describing life in England at the end of the 17th century. She is believed to be the person in the nursery rhyme:

'Ride a cock horse to Banbury Cross
To see a Fiennes lady on a white horse'

Mighty and Alison leave London and, covering about 25km a day, they clatter through East Anglia, across the Midlands and up through the Lake District to Carlisle. Then they cross over to Newcastle before heading south-west, via Banbury, to Bristol and into Cornwall. They reach Land's End on Sept. 22. After that, they turn back along the south coast through Winchester and up into London arriving back in Hyde Park on Oct. 22.

May 10:   PO issues 4 new stamps—Europa: Transport and Mail services in the 1930s

Friday *May 13*	A North American bison (Bison bison) is born at London Zoo to Minnie and Percy.
Saturday *May 14*	A police cadet team from the West Midlands comes first in the Ten Tors Trek across Dartmoor. Wimbledon beats Liverpool 1-0 in the FA Cup Final at Wembley.
Sunday *May 15*	Grenadier Guard Richard Stokes becomes the first black soldier to take up sentry duty outside Buckingham Palace. New Moon
Monday *May 16*	There is a plague of giant waterweed in Venice because of the mild winter and chemicals being washed down the River Po. Dredgers remove 508 tonnes from the canals today.
Tuesday *May 17*	Michael Jackson sings and dances for 60 seconds in the first advertisement for Pepsi-Cola on Russian television.
Wednesday *May 18*	The Pope celebrates his 68th birthday in Paraguay on the last day of his South American tour. The European Space Agency launches an *Ariane 2* rocket from French Guiana and puts a 2.03 tonne telecommunications satellite in orbit.
Thursday *May 19*	Wilberforce, the tabby cat who caught mice at No 10 Downing Street for 14yrs, dies peacefully in his sleep. New illuminations at Tower Bridge, London, are switched on.
Friday *May 20*	A special consignment of 20kg of yak hair for the helmets of the Blues and Royals of the Household Cavalry arrives at Heathrow from Peking. Yak Hair Yak Hair Yak Hair
Saturday *May 21*	Beginning of Wild Flower Week. Large clumps of reddish brown jelly, an algae called Chrysocyhromulina Polylepsis, ooze along the coasts of Denmark and Sweden at 24.14kph and suffocate the fish.
Sunday *May 22*	Jewish Festival of Weeks begins. Fire destroys 24 hectares of forest near Betws-y-Coed in the Snowdonia National Park.
Monday *May 23*	A large chemical cloud drifts over London and south east England. Robin Knox-Johnston relaunches *Suhaili*, the boat in which he sailed single-handed and non-stop around the world in 1968, to take part in the Trans-Atlantic yacht race which starts on June 5.
Tuesday *May 24*	The new £7,500,000 Tate Gallery in Albert Dock, Liverpool, is opened by the Prince of Wales. Snow falls in the Syrian desert.

Wednesday May 25	Princess Alexandra officially opens a formal hedge maze at Leeds Castle, Kent. It's a topiary castle with castellated yew hedges, an entrance bridge and a central tower.
Thursday May 26	Andrew Kendall (15), from Moreton, Merseyside, is named British Rail 'Super Traveller of the Year' after covering a record 176,837.93km last year. The Flower Festival at Stansted Mountfitchet Castle, Essex, is cancelled after a fallow deer called Clover eats most of the exhibits.
Friday May 27	Kay Cottee (34), from Australia, rounds the tip of southern Tasmania, on her 181st day at sea. She aims to be the first woman to sail round the world alone and non-stop.
Saturday May 28	A team of British climbers leaves England for the Himalayas: they will try to conquer Everest by the North East Ridge—the only route still unclimbed.
Sunday May 29	The Ystradgynlais Silver Band and Choir perform 106.68m underground in the Danyrogof Caves in the Brecon Beacons in front of an audience of 1000. Tiny Tim sets a world record in Brighton when he sings non-stop for 3hrs, 11mins.

Gales and heavy rain

Monday May 30	Bank Holiday. Telethon '88 raises £21,015,604 for children's charities.

Full Moon (the second this month)

Tuesday May 31	The new blue Smartie is born. Alison Payne sets off from Hyde Park, London, on Shire horse, Mighty, to ride round the country in aid of the Skin Treatment and Research Trust (START).

TOP TEN SINGLES*

1 The Only Way Is Up—Yazz and the Plastic Population
2 I Should Be So Lucky—Kylie Minogue
3 Mistletoe and Wine—Cliff Richard
4 I Think We're Alone Now—Tiffany
5 Especially For You—Kylie Minogue & Jason Donovan
6 Nothing's Gonna Change My Love For You—Glenn Medeiros
7 { With A Little Help From My Friends—Wet Wet Wet
7 { She's Leaving Home—Billy Bragg
8 The Locomotion—Kylie Minogue
9 He Ain't Heavy He's My Brother—The Hollies
10 Teardrops—Womack and Womack

(* According to *New Musical Express*)

TOP TEN FILMS*

1 Fatal Attraction
2 Crocodile Dundee II
3 Three Men and a Baby
4 A Fish Called Wanda
5 Coming To America
6 Good Morning, Vietnam
7 The Last Emperor
8 The Jungle Book
9 Buster
10 Beetlejuice

(* According to *Screen International*)

June

Wednesday June 1

'Kahyasi', owned by the Aga Khan, wins the 209th Derby at Epsom by 1½ lengths in 2mins 34secs.

Thursday June 2

35th anniversary of the Queen's Coronation. A rare Pallas's Rosefinch, which usually nests in USSR and winters in China or Japan, is spotted on the Scottish island of North Ronaldsay.

Friday June 3

A racing pigeon from Theale, Berks, which got lost on its way back from France and ended up on Jersey, is flown home by passenger airline.

Saturday June 4

René Bricka, who left Tenerife on April 1, arrives in Trinidad after walking 6,034.87km across the Atlantic on a pair of polyester floats. He hitched a lift from a Japanese freighter for the last 96.55km.

Sunday June 5

95 yachts set sail from Plymouth at the start of the Carlsberg single-handed Trans-Atlantic yacht race to Newport, Rhode Island, USA. Kay Cottee arrives back in Sydney, Australia, and becomes the first woman to sail alone non-stop round the world.

Monday June 6

A tablet in Poet's Corner, Westminster Abbey, is dedicated to the nonsense writer Edward Lear, who died 100 years ago. *The Owl and the Pussycat* is read and *The Pelican's Chorus* is sung at a special service.

Tuesday June 7

1 Bulgarian and 2 Soviet cosmonauts take off on a 10 day mission on board a *Soyuz* spacecraft for the orbiting *Mir* space station.

Wednesday June 8

A first edition of the comic *Beano*, dated July 30, 1938, priced at 2 old pence, is sold for £825 at an auction in Edinburgh.

Thursday June 9

A Great Peacock silk moth with a wingspan of 15.24cm is found at Wollaston, nr Wellingborough, Northants.

Friday June 10

The Princess of Wales unveils a plaque at the Women's International Tennis Association in London and then plays mixed doubles with Charles Swallow against Steffi Graf of Germany and Lord Willoughby de Broke. She loses 3-6 in a one set match.

Saturday June 11

Beginning of National Bike Week. A huge pop concert is held in Wembley Stadium in honour of the 70th birthday of Nelson Mandela, who is in prison in South Africa.

Sunday June 12

National Rambling Day. Jaguar comes first in the 24-hr motor race at Le Mans: it's the first British win for 31yrs.

June

Takes its name from Juno, the great Roman goddess of the Moon or from 'Juniores', the Latin word for young people, who were honoured this month. 'Zomer-maand' in Old Dutch (Summer month) and 'Seremonath' in Old Saxon (Dry month).

WATCH OUT! TERRIBLE DRAGONS ARRIVE AT THE NATURAL HISTORY MUSEUM IN LONDON!

In China the word for dinosaur is Konglong—or Terrible Dragon. This year a special delegation of dinosaur skeletons from China is visiting Britain. After 16 months at the National Museum of Wales in Cardiff, they are dismantled and the hundreds of bones (carefully numbered) are packed into crates. The museum's keeper of geology says 'We will miss them. The place will seem very empty'— not surprising, as one of the dinosaurs, the Mamenchisaurus is 22m long and the largest creature ever to walk the earth. They travel in convoy to London where it takes several weeks to unpack the bones and put them together again. The exhibition opens at the Natural History Museum on June 17.

Lufengosaurus	— more than 200,000,000 years old. It walked on its hind legs and was 6m long and 3m high. On the whole, it ate plants and just the occasional addition of small animals.
Mamenchisaurus	— the biggest dinosaur of all at 22m long. Its neck was 11m long and had 19 vertebrae. It walked on all fours and ate leaves and twigs.
Shunosaurus	— 170,000,000-year-old plant eater, which walked on all fours. It had teeth like combs which were excellent for stripping leaves off branches at great speed. It then swallowed them whole without chewing.
Gasosaurus	— a relative of Tyrannosaurus Rex and by far the most ferocious dinosaur in the exhibition. A meat eater with big teeth, it walked on its hind legs and was about 4m long and 2m high.
Tuojiangosaurus	— 155,000,000-years-old, with a tiny head and a double row of bony back plates. Some people think these were a kind of armour, others that they helped to keep the creature warm—rather like solar panels.
Tsintaosaurus	— 90,000,000-year-old plant eater, 8m long and 4m high, which walked on its back legs. It had a bony crest on top of its head rather like a unicorn's horn.

Monday *June 13*	The lighthouse at Happisburgh, Norfolk, which was built in 1791, is switched off for the last time. A school of 20 whales attacks and sinks a yacht called *Hyccup* about 1609km out to sea in the Trans-Atlantic yacht race.
Tuesday *June 14*	Opening Day of Royal Ascot. A lifeboat called the *Jessie Lumb*, which rescued pilots shot down in the Channel during the Battle of Britain in World War II, goes back to the Imperial War Museum at Duxford, Cambs, after restoration.

25°C in central Scotland　　　　　New Moon

Wednesday *June 15*	The European Space Agency's newest rocket, *Ariane 4* is launched on her maiden flight from French Guiana. Philippe Poupon wins the single-handed Trans-Atlantic yacht race in 18.2m trimaran *Fleury Michon IX* in a record 10 days 9hrs 15mins 19secs.
Thursday *June 16*	25 years ago today, Valentina Tereshkova became the first woman in space when she made 48 orbits of Earth in *Vostok 6*.
Friday *June 17*	A special exhibition of Chinese dinosaurs opens at the Natural History Museum, London. Geoff Cooper sets off from Gweek, Cornwall, to row around the world in his 4.88m boat *Water Rat*.
Saturday *June 18*	Tonight the coast of Australia sparkles with more than 500 beacons, lit to celebrate 200 years of European settlement.
Sunday *June 19*	Father's Day. Ruby, a piranha (6), wins Best in Show title at the 1988 Fishkeeping Exhibition in Esher, Surrey.
Monday *June 20*	National Dance Week. The first British pub opens in Moscow: it's called Krasney Lev (The Red Lion).

Heavy showers and thunderstorms with hail in East Anglia

Tuesday *June 21*	Sioux medicine man 'Crow Dog' finishes his 3-day rain dance in Clyde, Ohio, USA to help end the worst drought this century.
Wednesday *June 22*	The Periwinkle Cottage Tearooms, Selworthy Green, nr Porlock, Somerset, is named Top Tea Place of the Year by the Tea Council.
Thursday *June 23*	7mm of rain falls in Clyde, Ohio (see June 21). Geoff Cooper, who set off on Friday from Gweek, Cornwall, to row around the world is rescued 74km south of the Lizard and towed to France.
Friday *June 24*	Midsummer's Day. The largest solar flare for 4yrs lasts for more than 1½ hours. 3000 racing pigeons set off from Bourges, central France, at 5.20am for the north of England.

Saturday *June 25*	The Netherlands beat the Soviet Union 2-0 in the final of the European Soccer Championship at Munich. The first pigeon that left France yesterday arrives back in Newbiggin, Northumberland (933.39km) at 8.30am.
Sunday *June 26*	Teams from 27 countries take part in the 13th Hong Kong International Dragon Boat Races. Dave Hurst, from Stockport, and Alan Matthews, from Hebburn, Tyne and Wear, become the first blind men to climb Mont Blanc, the highest mountain in Europe. 
Monday *June 27*	The Motor Vehicles (Wearing of Rear Seat Belts by Children) Bill is approved by the House of Lords. Sky-scrapers sway in San Francisco during an earthquake that measures 5.2 on the Richter Scale.
Tuesday *June 28*	17 British beaches win the EEC Blue Flag for being clean and safe. The birthplace of Thomas Bewick, the famous engraver and naturalist, at Cherryburn nr Newcastle, is opened by the Queen Mother.
Wednesday *June 29*	Dray horses Washington and Windsor start their 2-week summer holiday at a hop farm at Beltring, near Paddock Wood, Kent. Full Moon
Thursday *June 30*	It's been the driest June for 12yrs in England and Wales. 2nd Punch and Judy Championships at Mablethorpe, Lincs, is won by Prof. Pieman Nobody.

June 21:
PO issues 4 new stamps to celebrate the Bicentenary of Australian Settlement

The Herald
BRITISH BEACHES WHICH WIN THE EEC BLUE FLAG FOR BEING SAFE & CLEAN: TORBAY, CRINNIS, POOLE, PORTHMEOR, BLACKPOOL SANDS, EXMOUTH, LEE-ON-SOLENT, SIDMOUTH, WEYMOUTH, STOKES BAY, BOURNEMOUTH, PEMBERRY

The Trumpet
1,000 YEARS OF CHRISTIANITY CELEBRATED IN SOVIET UNION

Bleet
BRITISH DORMOUSE BECOMES ENDANGERED SPECIES
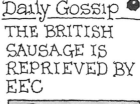

Daily Gossip
THE BRITISH SAUSAGE IS REPRIEVED BY EEC
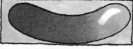

July

Friday July 1

Greece takes on the presidency of the EEC. Happy 27th birthday to the Princess of Wales—and to Carl Lewis, who won 4 gold medals at the Los Angeles Olympics in 1984.

Saturday July 2

The World Custard Pie Championship is held at Ditton Park, Maidstone. Steffi Graf (19) beats Martina Navratilova (31) 5-7, 6-2, 6-1, to win the Women's Singles Championship at Wimbledon.

Sunday July 3

A Royal Marines team from 539 Assault Squadron finishes a 2,413.95km journey round the coast of Britain in an inflatable boat. It took them 3 days, 17hrs—a new world record.

Monday July 4

Independence Day in the USA. The Teddy Bear Museum in Stratford-upon-Avon is officially opened. Stefan Edberg (22) beats Boris Becker (20) 4-6, 7-6, 6-4, 6-2, to win the Men's Singles Championship at Wimbledon, after the match was delayed by torrential rain yesterday.

Tuesday July 5

The National Health Service celebrates its 40th birthday. Karl Bowers becomes the first person to drive a battery-powered vehicle non-stop round the M25. It takes him 3hrs at 64kph.

Wednesday July 6

A huge explosion destroys the 34,544 tonne oil platform 'Piper Alpha' in the North Sea—the worst off-shore oil rig disaster in history.

Thursday July 7

Tottenham Hotspur pays Newcastle United £2,000,000 for Paul Gascoigne. The Soviet Union launches an unmanned spacecraft to Mars, to investigate one of its tiny moons called Phobos (fear). Christopher Marshall (11) leaves San Diego, California, to fly a single-engine aircraft 11,364.88km across the US and Atlantic.

Friday July 8

'Sci-Tech I', a cardboard rocket made by pupils at Acton High School, is launched at Shoeburyness, Essex. It reaches 152.4m. Marilyn Monroe's autograph fetches £1,000 in Nottingham.

Saturday July 9

Mrs Denise St Aubyn Hubbard (64) becomes the oldest woman to sail the Atlantic alone, when she arrives at Newport, Rhode Island, after 34 days in the Trans-Atlantic Yacht Race.

Sunday July 10

A gigantic 21.34m model of Jonathan Swift's Gulliver arrives in Dublin as part of the city's 1000th birthday celebrations. Mrs Margaret Rogers, from Devizes, Wilts, wins the National Scrabble Championship in London.

Monday July 11

The National Museum of Photography, Film and Television in Bradford wins the Museum of the Year Award for 1988.

July

Named in honour of Julius Caesar. Also known as 'the yellow month' (Gaelic) and 'the month of the midsummer moon' (Anglo Saxon).

July 19:

PO issues 5 new stamps to commemorate the 400th anniversary of the defeat of the Spanish Armada

ARMADA · NORTH SEA · 30 JULY - 2 AUG 1588

ARMADA · LIZARD · 19 JULY 1588   ARMADA · PLYMOUTH · 21 JULY 1588   ARMADA · ISLE of WIGHT · 25 JULY 1588   ARMADA · CALAIS · 28-29 JULY 1588

SWAN-UPPING ON THE RIVER THAMES

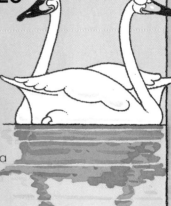

Long ago the swan was a very useful source of fresh meat as it paddled up and down the river Thames. It was, however, a licensed royal bird, which meant that you had to have special permission from the King or Queen before you caught a swan for Sunday lunch.

Lots of the old livery companies used to hold licences enabling them to catch swans, but now only two do—the Dyers and the Vintners. Together with the Queen they are responsible for all the mute swans on the river Thames. The Dyers and Vintners still hold traditional Swan Feasts in the City of London every year—although the menu hasn't included swan for a long time.

Every year, in the third week in July, the Royal Swan Keeper counts the swans between Sunbury and Pangbourne and shares out the new cygnets. So that they don't get in a muddle he marks their beaks—one nick on the right hand side for a Dyers' bird, two nicks (one on either side) for a Vintners' bird and no mark at all for the Queen's birds.

This year 25 broods are found and marked, with a total of 102 cygnets. Half are given to the Queen (56 cygnets), the Dyers get 29 and the Vintners 27.

FIRE OVER ENGLAND—JULY 19

The first beacon is lit at 10.10pm at Kynance Cove on the Lizard, Cornwall, where the Spanish Armada was first sighted as it sailed towards England in 1588. It takes about 28 minutes for 460 more beacons all over the country to be set ablaze. They stretch from Cornwall to Berwick-upon-Tweed and from Essex to North Wales.

Tuesday *July 12*	The Fresh Fruit and Vegetable Information Bureau says that a 3cm wide Black Widow spider has been found on Californian grapes at Southampton.
Wednesday *July 13*	A fund to raise money for guide dogs is launched in memory of Teddy, who died last week. He was the guide dog of David Blunkett, Labour MP for Sheffield Brightside. New Moon
Thursday *July 14*	Christopher Marshall (11) lands at Paris after flying his single-engine aircraft 11,364.88km across the US and the Atlantic, retracing Charles Lindbergh's flight in 1927. 10°C at Cape Wrath
Friday *July 15*	St Swithin's Day: if it rains today, it will be wet for the next 40 days. There are showers all over the country! The 6th European Hang Gliding Championships in north east Italy end a day early because the Pope is on holiday nearby.
Saturday *July 16*	61 yachts take part in a race from San Sebastian, Spain, to Plymouth, Devon, to commemorate the 400th anniversary of the defeat of the Spanish Armada. Florence Joyner runs the fastest women's 100m ever in 10.49secs at Indianapolis, USA.
Sunday *July 17*	The Annual World Snail Championship is held at Congham, Norfolk: Tracker, who belongs to Robert High (6), from Grimston, wins after completing the 33.02cm course in 2mins, 31secs.
Monday *July 18*	The ancient yearly tradition of Swan-Upping starts on the River Thames at Windsor. Over the next four days the Queen's Swan Keeper will count and mark this season's cygnets.
Tuesday *July 19*	The Spanish Ambassador lights the first of 461 beacons all over England at the Lizard, Cornwall, as part of the Armada celebrations.
Wednesday *July 20*	Michael Jackson visits the children in Great Ormond Street Hospital, London. Car number plate NEW 1 is sold for £17,600 at Phillips saleroom in London. NEW 1
Thursday *July 21*	The Queen and the Duke of Edinburgh watch a re-enactment of William of Orange's landing at Brixham, Devon, in 1688. Fenberry Catalina, from Nottinghamshire, is named Pig of the Year at the East of England Show, Peterborough.
Friday *July 22*	The London Pavilion in Piccadilly Circus, London, re-opens today. Sue Broughton, from Hungerford, Berks, receives the National Librarian of the Year Award at the House of Commons.

Saturday *July 23*	The 102nd Annual Olympian Games are held at Much Wenlock, Shropshire. Today's events include swimming and fencing. The giant drill which started digging the Channel Tunnel at the end of last year is now 1,495.04m out from Dover.
Sunday *July 24*	The Prince of Wales opens the 1988 National Wheelchair Games in Buckinghamshire.
Monday *July 25*	Pilgrims arrive at Santiago de Compostela, Spain, for the Feast of St James—including Charles Paternina and Paul Graham who set off 6 weeks ago from London on pennyfarthing bicycles.
Tuesday *July 26*	Laurent Smagghe, from France, sets a new record by running up and down the highest peak in Europe, Mont Blanc, 4,810.04m in 6hrs, 16mins. (See July 28).
Wednesday *July 27*	Mercury Communications open their first payphones at Waterloo Station, London. 10 motorists in Nottinghamshire become the first to be fined for jumping a red light after being photographed by remote-controlled cameras.
Thursday *July 28*	Jacques Berlie, from Switzerland, claims a new record by running up and down Mont Blanc, the highest mountain in Europe, in 5hrs, 37mins and 56secs.
Friday *July 29*	Full Moon Defeat of the Spanish Armada 1588. A huge silver soup tureen in the shape of a turtle is sold for £9,350 at Phillips' saleroom in London.
Saturday *July 30*	Special 50th birthday edition (No. 2402) of the comic *Beano* goes on sale, price 20p. Competitors from America and Europe take part in the 3rd Annual Yogic Flying Competition in Skelmersdale, Lancs.
Sunday *July 31*	Brian Letcomber loops the loop 180 times at Plymouth and sets a new world record. The annual whale count ends in Norway. They spot a school of 11 blue whales, the first to be seen in Norwegian waters for 30yrs.

Grapevine ★

POLICE CANCEL FIRST CANNONBALL RUN ROUND M.25

Chatterbox ●

FRENCH COMPANY BUYS HP SAUCE

Newsreel ▲

CRATERS ON MOON NAMED AFTER US ASTRONAUTS KILLED IN SHUTTLE DISASTER IN 1986

Good Egg ◗

US WARSHIP SHOOTS DOWN IRANIAN AIRLINER IN GULF

August

Monday
August 1

F is the new letter at the beginning of car number plates from today. Nottingham declares a new litter-free zone and appoints a full-time Litter Warden.

Tuesday
August 2

T. James Jones, from Newcastle Emlyn, Dyfed, is crowned Bard of the National Eisteddfod in Newport, Gwent.

Wednesday
August 3

A Tristram's Storm Petrel from the Pacific Ocean is spotted off the Cornish coast near Newlyn. It has never been seen in the Atlantic before. A Beatrix Potter watercolour from *The Tale of Pigling Bland* is sold for £5,500 at Christie's, South Kensington.

Thursday
August 4

41 gun salutes from Hyde Park and the Tower of London to wish the Queen Mother Happy 88th Birthday. The orb on the spire of the central tower at the Palace of Westminster is taken down to be repaired and regilded.

Friday
August 5

The Prince of Wales opens the new National Waterways Museum in Gloucester. British parachutist Michael McCarthy jumps off the 54.56m Leaning Tower of Pisa in Italy and claims a world record for a low-level jump from a building.

Saturday
August 6

52 contestants take part in the 37th National Town Criers' Championship at St Leonard's on Sea. The Great Armada Pageant along the River Thames recreates Queen Elizabeth I's visit to Tilbury in 1588 to inspect her army. Hot and sunny

Sunday
August 7

Harry Taylor (GB), and Russell Brice (NZ), conquer Mt Everest's north east ridge, which has never been climbed before. Oliver Holmes, Richard Barr and John Derricott make the first hot-air balloon crossing of the North Sea in 18hrs from Mintlaw, nr Aberdeen, to Copenhagen, Denmark. 29°C at Great Malvern

Monday
August 8

The Duchess of York gives birth to a daughter at 8.18pm at the Portland Hospital, London. Teiichi Igarashi (101) reaches the top of the highest mountain in Japan, 3,774.94m Mount Fuji, after a 3-day climb.

Tuesday
August 9

The first stage of the Kellogg's Tour of Britain cycle race starts in Newcastle-upon-Tyne. A 41 gun salute is fired in London to welcome the new Royal Princess.

Wednesday
August 10

A special international conference is held in London to discuss the mystery disease that has killed more than 6000 seals in the North Sea. Australian, Rik Dunkan, hang-glides down Mount Fuji (3,774.94m), the highest mountain in Japan. It takes him about 1hr.

August

Named in honour of the Roman Emperor Augustus, whose lucky month it was. Also known as 'harvest month' and 'weed month'.

The Olympic Flame

August 23

Hera's Temple, Olympia, Greece

The Olympic Flame is kindled from the sun's rays

August 24

The sacred flame is carried by a relay of torch bearers to Athens (380 km)

August 25

Athens
Pan-Athenian Stadium
6pm

The flame is handed over to officials from Seoul in an hour long ceremony

August 26

It flies by chartered jet to Cheju Island in S. Korea, stopping for refuelling in Bahrain and Bangkok

August 27

Cheju Island, South Korea
11am

The flame arrives to official welcoming ceremonies and is then shipped to Pusan on the mainland

August 28

Torch bearers start a 4.066 km 22-day relay run across S. Korea to Seoul

September 17

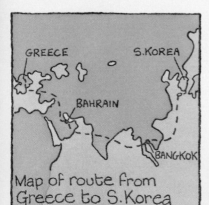

Map of route from Greece to S. Korea

The Olympic Flame arrives in Seoul for the opening ceremony

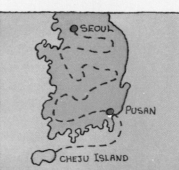

Map of the torch relay route through S. Korea

Thursday *August 11*	The best night of the year to see the Perseid meteor shower—especially because there is no moonlight.
Friday *August 12*	Start of the grouse shooting season. Earthquake in Tokyo measures 5.3 on Richter Scale.
Saturday *August 13*	163 hot-air balloons finally take off in the 10th International Fiesta at Bristol despite heavy rain and strong winds. One crashes onto the roof of a swimming pool.
Sunday *August 14*	Islamic New Year (AH 1409). 40 competitors take part in the International Birdman Rally, Bognor Regis, Sussex. Malcolm Elliott, from Sheffield, wins the final stage of the Kellogg's Tour of Britain cycle race in Westminster.
Monday *August 15*	Vijay Singhania takes off from London's Dockland Airport in an attempt to break the 34-day microlight record from London to Bombay. The first new European-style British passports are issued in Glasgow.
Tuesday *August 16*	A 2.72kg salmon is caught in the River Thames at Bell Weir, Egham, Surrey.
Wednesday *August 17*	Dani Maimone, from Bingham, Notts., sets a new British hot-air balloon altitude record of 5,882.664m. Harry 'Butch' Reynolds, from the US, sets a new world record for the 400m in Zurich with a time of 43.29secs.
Thursday *August 18*	'A' level results come out today: Ganesh Sittampalam (9), from Surbiton, becomes the youngest pupil ever to get an A grade in Maths 'A' level.
Friday *August 19*	Steve Cram runs the fastest 1500m in the world this year with a time of 3mins 30.97secs in Brussels. A section of the M2 in Kent is closed by motorway police so that a swan can take off.
Saturday *August 20*	133 competitors take part in the 17th Isle of Man World Tin Bath Championships. You can pick your own blackberries on the Queen's fruit farm as Sandringham for 40p per 453.59g.
Sunday *August 21*	A powerful earthquake in the foothills of the Himalayas, on the borders of India and Nepal, measures 6.7 on the Richter Scale. It shakes an area from Kashmir to Bangladesh.
Monday *August 22*	The Duke and Duchess of York name their daughter (born August 8) Beatrice Elizabeth Mary.

New Moon

Tuesday *August 23*	The Olympic Flame is lit at the Temple of Hera at Olympia in Greece. The first of 350 runners starts the torch relay across Greece to Seoul in South Korea for the opening ceremony of the Games on September 17.
Wednesday *August 24*	Bert Bissell (86) from Dudley, Yorks, climbs to the top of Ben Nevis, Scotland, for the 100th time. He first climbed it in 1932. A white one-piece 'Shooting Star' suit that belonged to Elvis Presley is sold for £28,600 at Phillips saleroom in London.
Thursday *August 25*	The first GCSE exam results come out today. An autographed pair of Michael Jackson's dancing shoes is sold for £3000 at Christie's.
Friday *August 26*	Lynne Cox, from the US, takes 4hrs, 20mins to swim 17.38km across Lake Baikal in Siberia. The water temperature is 11°C.
Saturday *August 27*	Full Moon Kevin Murphy, from Harrow, is the only competitor to finish the Loch Lomond Marathon Swim in heavy rain and gale force winds. It takes him 13hrs, 57mins, 56secs to complete the 37.01km course.
Sunday *August 28*	The Notting Hill Carnival in London starts today. A 14.02m long, 77.21 tonne Southern Right Whale swims into Botany Bay, Australia.
Monday *August 29*	Bank Holiday. Matthew Sadler (14), from Rochester, Kent, becomes the youngest British player to be named as a chess International Master.
Tuesday *August 30*	The largest aircraft in the world, the Soviet Antonov 124 transport plane, arrives at Farnborough, Hants, for the air show.
Wednesday *August 31*	The Afghan-Soviet space mission, which left Earth on Monday, docks with the orbiting space station *Mir*. On board is a doctor who will check the health of the 2 cosmonauts who have been in space since last December.

Town Crier ▲
BOMB EXPLODES AT MILL HILL BARRACKS

The Owl ◯
SHARK WITH GLOW-IN-THE-DARK LIPS WASHED UP IN W. AUSTRALIA

Sensation ☆
NEW BUDDHIST TEMPLE INAUGURATED AT ESKDALEMUIR, SCOTLAND

Daily Lemon
GOODBYE TO CLOVELLY LIFEBOAT AFTER 118 YEARS

September

Thursday *September 1*	Gales, heavy rain and floods: the hovercraft *Prince of Wales* has its skirt ripped and is towed into Dover. Giant Panda Chia-Chia (16) leaves London Zoo for the USA, on his way to meet his new mate Tohui in Mexico City Zoo.
Friday *September 2*	The £24,000,000 Australian Telescope, the largest radio telescope in the southern hemisphere, is officially unveiled in Culgoora.
Saturday *September 3*	The Denby Dale Bicentenary Pie is baked in Yorkshire. it's the biggest meat and potato pie in the world.
Sunday *September 4*	Paul Woodruff, from Camden, wins the London Taxi Driver of the Year competition in Battersea Park.
Monday *September 5*	Cosmonauts Vladimir Lyakhov and Abdul Ahad leave the orbiting space station *Mir* on their *Soyuz TM-5* landing craft and head back to Earth.
Tuesday *September 6*	Thomas Gregory (11yrs, 11mnths) from Eltham, London, becomes the youngest person ever to swim the English Channel. It takes him 12hrs to cross from Cap Gris Nez to Dover.
Wednesday *September 7*	150yrs ago today a lighthouse keeper's daughter called Grace Darling rowed out to sea and saved 9 people from a shipwreck on Farne Island, off the Northumbrian coast.
Thursday *September 8*	Vijay Singhania sets a new London–India microlight record when he lands in Bombay after a 22-day flight.
Friday *September 9*	Start of Green Consumer Week: a new planet-friendly aerosol, using no hydrocarbons or fluorocarbons, is launched.
Saturday *September 10*	A statue of Sherlock Holmes is unveiled by members of the Sherlock Holmes Society at Meiringen, nr the Reichenbach Falls, Switzerland. New Moon
Sunday *September 11*	50,000,000 people in 128 different countries take part in the 2nd Sport Aid 'Race Against Time' to raise money for children in need.
Monday *September 12*	Jewish New Year (AM 5749). 2 earth tremors nr Ambleside in the Lake District measure 3 on the Richter Scale.
Tuesday *September 13*	Hurricane Gilbert hits the Cayman Islands and Jamaica in the Caribbean at 257.49kph, leaving 60,000 people homeless. It's so strong that it is designated a Category 5 hurricane—only the third this century.

Wednesday *September 14*	Day of the Holy Nut—beginning of the nutting season. Michael Werikhe, from Kenya, reaches London at the end of a 2,896.74km sponsored walk through 5 countries in aid of the black rhinoceros.
Thursday *September 15*	UNICEF's World Children's Week is launched today. The Museum of the Moving Image (MOMI) is opened on the South Bank, London, by the Prince of Wales.
Friday *September 16*	A 67.06m gas tank, which weighs 127 tonnes, travels along the M27 on 96 wheels to BP's oilfield at Poole Harbour, Dorset.
Saturday *September 17*	Chinese Moon Festival. More than 12,000 dancers, 1,000 taekwondo fighters and 32 sky divers forming the Olympic emblem open the games of the XXIV Olympiad at Seoul, S. Korea.
Sunday *September 18*	A rare American Golden Plover is spotted near Pagham Harbour, W. Sussex. Kuwait lifts a 21yr ban on Coca-Cola.

September

This was the seventh month of the year in the old Roman calendar when the year used to start in March. Also known as the 'month of reaping', 'barley month' and the 'holy month'.

THE DENBY DALE BICENTENARY PIE

The Denby Dale Bicentenary Pie contains 2800kg Prime English Beef, 2800kg potatoes, 700kg onions, 700kg gravy and special seasoning, 1500kg flour and 1200kg margarine. The gigantic pie dish measures 6.5 × 2.25m, and is 0.55m deep. It's the biggest meat and potato pie ever baked and celebrates 200 years of huge pie-making in Denby Dale.

How It is Cooked
The meat and potato filling is cooked in special steam kettles in $\frac{1}{4}$-tonne batches. It is then spread into 12 trays which fit neatly into one enormous tray—with just enough room between them for hot water to circulate and keep the food nice and warm. The pie crust, which is only for decoration, is supported on 6 sections of metal mesh. Other puff pastry is pre-baked in 50 gram portions and re-heated in a travelling oven just before serving.

It started with the George III Pie, in 1788 to celebrate the King's return to his senses, and was followed in 1815 by the Victory Pie, which marked Wellington's victory over Napoleon at Waterloo.

The Village Hall Pie of 1964, contained 3 tonnes of beef, 1.5 tonnes potatoes and 15 tonnes of gravy and seasoning. 30,000 portions were sold and helped to raise money for a special Pie Hall.

Monday *September 19*	Adrian Moorhouse (24) wins Britain's first gold medal at the Seoul Olympics in the 100m breast-stroke. £2,000,000 Eurotunnel Exhibition Centre is opened at Folkestone, Kent.
Tuesday *September 20*	The Alternative Olympics are held in Hull. The Prince of Wales joins the campaign to protect endangered Barn Owls by giving free owl nesting boxes to his tenants in the Duchy of Cornwall.
Wednesday *September 21*	Yom Kippur—the Jewish Day of Atonement. Sean Crowley, from Croydon, arrives at Clifden, Co. Galway, after rowing his 6.40m boat 3,701.39km across the Atlantic Ocean from Halifax, Nova Scotia, in 96 days.
Thursday *September 22*	A huge leatherback turtle is washed up on Harlech beach in Wales. It weighs 907kg, is 251cms wide and 288cms long.
Friday *September 23*	A new planet that was first spotted in 1979 is named after Len Carter, Secretary of the British Interplanetary Society for 50yrs.
Saturday *September 24*	A new ring of 13 bells, made of metal from Australia, is inaugurated at St Martin-in-the-Fields, London. A new training centre for Hearing Dogs for the Deaf is opened at Lewknor, Oxfordshire.
Sunday *September 25*	Nearly 30,000 athletes, including Olympic champions Herb Elliott and Emil Zatopeck, take part in the 4.02km *Sunday Times* Fun Run in Hyde Park, London. Full Moon
Monday *September 26*	Cargo vessel *Ardlough* sinks in storms in the Irish Sea.
Tuesday *September 27*	More than 30 warships take part in a special week-long Bicentennial Naval Salute in Sydney Harbour, Australia.
Wednesday *September 28*	More than 2,000 people arrive for the 52nd annual convention of the International Brotherhood of Magicians at Brighton.
Thursday *September 29*	US space shuttle *Discovery* lifts off with a 5-man crew from Cape Canaveral and goes into orbit 296.11km above Earth. 20 tonnes of biscuits are washed ashore at Blackpool from the *Ardlough*, which sank in the Irish Sea on Monday.
Friday *September 30*	ERNIE 3 is born: his full name is Electronic Random Number Indicator Equipment and his job is to choose the lucky Premium Bonds.

-3.8°C at Carnwath, Srtathclyde

October

This was the eighth month in the old Roman calendar when the year started in March. It has also been known as 'wine month' and 'month of the winter moon'.

Saturday October 1
There's a firework spectacular and a Dragon Race in Cardiff Bay today to celebrate the re-opening of Cardiff Docks. 32 whales are rescued after they beach themselves in Augusta, Western Australia.

Sunday October 2
The games of the XXIV Olympiad close in Seoul, South Korea. The next Games will be in Barcelona, Spain, in 1992.

Monday October 3
Admission charges are introduced for the first time ever at the Science Museum, London: £2 for adults, £1 for children.

Tuesday October 4
6 North Sea oil rigs are shut down after a gas leak is discovered on board the Ninian Central platform, 160.93km NE of the Shetlands.

Wednesday October 5
Richard Brown, from London, reaches John O'Groats after running from Land's End in 10 days, 18hrs and 23mins, averaging 112.65km a day.

Thursday October 6
65 countries agree to ban the burning of chemicals at sea by the end of 1994.

Friday October 7
Eskimos discover 3 California Gray Whales trapped beneath the ice off Point Barrow in North Alaska, and cut air holes to help them breathe.

Saturday October 8
A huge laser concert in Royal Victoria Dock, London, closes the river to commercial traffic for the first time. The floating stage is made out of 12 barges and measures 36.4m × 27.3m.

Sunday October 9
Will Cox, from Honiton, Devon, wins the World Conker championship at Ashton, nr Oundle, Northants.

Monday October 10
The Special Boat Squadron and the RN minesweeper HMS *Nurton* arrive in Brighton as part of a gigantic security operation for the Conservative Party Conference, which opens tomorrow. New Moon

Tuesday October 11
The epidemic of canine distemper, which has devastated seal colonies in the North Sea this year, reaches the Firth of Clyde.

Wednesday October 12
Jacqui Noble, Paul Scott and Fitzgerald Weeks finish driving round the coast of Britain (5,880km) in a record 2 days, 15hrs, 49mins.

Thursday October 13
A giant swarm of locusts, which stretches for more than 643km, arrives in Saudi Arabia from Sudan and Ethiopia.

Friday *October 14*	Pupils from Old Oak Primary School, West London, plant 33 acorns and oak saplings on Wormwood Scrubs to mark the first anniversary of the Great Storm last year.
Saturday *October 15*	242 disabled competitors take part in the Paralympics, which open in Seoul, South Korea, today. Donald Campbell's record-breaking car *Bluebird* goes on display at the British Museum, London.
Sunday *October 16*	A candlelit procession to St Peter's, Rome, celebrates the Pope's 10th year in office.
Monday *October 17*	Jason Bunn, Britain's Monopoly World Champion, loses his title to Japanese Ikuo Hiyakuta at the finals in London. An earthquake in Greece measures 6.5 on the Richter Scale
Tuesday *October 18*	A 20.18kg pike is caught in the Llandegfedd trout reservoir near Pontypool, Gwent. 21.5°C at East Malling, Kent
Wednesday *October 19*	US mounts a huge rescue operation to save three California Gray Whales trapped by Arctic ice off North Alaska. The Eskimos have named them Pouto (Ice Hole), Siku (Ice) and Kannick (Snowflake).
Thursday *October 20*	For Sale: *Happy Birthday To You*. Offers to the Sengstack family of New Jersey, who own the copyright. Happy Birthday To You

THE SEOUL OLYMPICS
Sept. 17 – Oct. 2

Tennis and table tennis are added to the menu of official Olympic sports this year. This means that there are now 23 different sports on the Olympic programme—at the first modern Games in Athens in 1896 there were only 10.

OLYMPIC SPORTS '88
(with the year that they were first included)

Archery (1900)	Football (Association) (1900)	Swimming (1896)
Athletics (1896)	Gymnastics (1896)	Table Tennis (1988)
Basketball (1936)	Handball (1972)	Tennis (1988)
Boxing (1904)	Hockey (1908)	Volleyball (1964)
Canoeing (1936)	Judo (1964)	Weightlifting (1896)
Cycling (1896)	Modern Pentathlon (1912)	Wrestling (1896)
Equestrianism (1900)	Rowing (1900)	Yachting (1900)
Fencing (1896)	Shooting (1896)	

SOME EX-OLYMPIC SPORTS
(with the year that they were dropped)

Cricket (1900)	Motor Boating (1908)	Golf (1900)
Croquet (1900)	Polo (1936)	Lacrosse (1908)
Rugby (1924)	Standing Jump (1912)	Tug of War (1920)

Friday *October 21*	Britain's first space centre, at Leicester University, is inaugurated by the Education Secretary, Kenneth Baker.
Saturday *October 22*	Hurricane Joan hits Nicaragua at 274kph and causes £452,000,000 damage. Alison Payne and Shire horse Mighty arrive back in London after their 2,574.88km Great Journey round England in aid of charity. (See May 31).
Sunday *October 23*	British Summer Time ends at 2am when clocks go back an hour. Christmas lights go up in Bristol. Alexander (9) and Lorelei (7) Harwood, from Cirencester, Gloucs, are chosen as Bisto Kids of the Year.
Monday *October 24*	2 Soviet ice-breaking ships join the US whale-saving team in Alaska (see Oct 19). The Seoul Paralympics close with British athletes winning 29 medals. Bob Matthews, from Rochester, Kent, won 3 gold medals for the 800m, 1,500m and 5,000m races for the blind.
Tuesday *October 25*	Andrew Quatermain (13), from Ipswich, wins the Choirboy of the Year competition in London. Full Moon
Wednesday *October 26*	2 of the California Gray whales, trapped for nearly 3 weeks in Arctic ice, are freed after rescuers cut a channel to the open sea. The third whale has disappeared.
Thursday *October 27*	Guy Smith arrives at the Sydney Opera House having driven his black London taxi 22,530.2km from Buckingham Palace. It took him 70 days and the fare on the meter is £31,445!
Friday *October 28*	Two driverless 101.60 tonne locomotives crash down an embankment onto the North Circular Road in London at the junction with the M1 at Staples Corner.
Saturday *October 29*	Sebastian Coe wins an historic 359m race against Steve Cram round Great Court, Trinity College, Cambridge in 45.052secs while the clock strikes 12. It is just within the 45.20secs it takes the clock to chime.
Sunday *October 30*	The official recorder of jumping insects in Britain reports that 5 desert locusts have been found in Cornwall and one in the Scilly Is.
Monday *October 31*	Hallowe'en. A new 203.2 tonne steel bridge across the River Twyi in Wales is opened to replace the old one that collapsed a year ago. There have been a record 156 earthquakes in Greece this month.

November

Tuesday November 1
New Forest ponies are fitted with glow-in-the-dark neckbands so that drivers can see them at night.

Wednesday November 2
A computer 'worm' is discovered in a US Defence Department system in California.

Thursday November 3
A Penny Black stamp, dating from 1840, is sold for £71,500 at Phillips saleroom, London. Watch out for the Taurids meteor shower tonight!

Friday November 4
The Queen unveils a plaque in York Minster, to celebrate its restoration after being badly damaged by lightning 4 years ago.

Saturday November 5
Bonfire Night. The new North Devon Link Road between Tiverton and Newtown is opened this week—complete with 800 wolves eyes (special reflectors) to scare away wild deer.

Sunday November 6
An 1899 Marot-Gardon tricycle finishes first out of 427 competitors in the London to Brighton veteran car race.

Monday November 7
The Christmas lights are switched on in Regent Street, London. Children at Penton Primary School, Islington, open a Time Capsule buried under a new wing of the local Fever Hospital in 1928.

Tuesday November 8
Rare wading birds, including Avocets, Brent Geese and Oyster Catchers, are threatened after 22,730 litres of oil spills into the River Clyst in Devon.

Wednesday November 9
A 4.85kg lemon, grown in a greenhouse at the Lackham College of Agriculture, Wilts, sets a new world record.

New Moon

Thursday November 10
A common seal called Godzilla (4), swims out to sea from Hunstanton, Norfolk, after recovering from a deadly virus at the Seal Assessment Centre, Docking.

Friday November 11
Soviet cosmonauts Vladimir Titov and Musa Manarov break the space endurance record after 326 days on board the orbiting space station *Mir*.

Saturday November 12
Lord Mayor's Show. Shire horse Mighty, who has just come back from his Great Journey all round England, helps to pull the Lord Mayor's golden coach through the City of London.

Sunday November 13
Remembrance Sunday. Hundreds of people are evacuated from their homes on the Isle of Dogs after an unexploded 226.8kg bomb from World War II is found near Poplar station, East London.

Monday *November 14*	Happy 40th Birthday to the Prince of Wales! The Department of the Environment announces that butterflies, including the Large Copper and the Duke of Burgundy Fritillary, are to be given special protection.
Tuesday *November 15*	The new independent state of Palestine is born at 1.40am. The first unmanned Soviet space shuttle *Buran* (Snowstorm) takes off and orbits Earth twice in a flight of 3hrs, 25mins.

November

This was the ninth month of the Roman calendar when the year started in March. The old Saxon name was 'wind-monath'—wind month. The old Dutch name was 'slaght-maand'—slaughter month.

The Time Capsule

The 60-year-old Time Capsule opened on Nov 7, contains 11 coins, a copy of *The Times* and a letter from the then hospital authorities, apologising for the delay in building. Although the jar was buried in 1928, the hospital wing was not actually finished until 1936. After the capsule is emptied, it is refilled with a £1 coin, a credit card, a digital watch, a book of 1988 Christmas stamps, an account by one of the children of the opening ceremony and a copy of the *Islington Gazette*. This new 1988 Time Capsule is then reburied by the Duke of Gloucester in the foundations of a local housing project.

November 15:

PO issues 5 new Christmas stamps

Wednesday *November 16*	Hereford Cathedral decides to sell the *Mappa Mundi*, a precious 13th century map of the world, drawn on a single sheet of vellum. It causes public uproar.
Thursday *November 17*	340,000,000-year-old Lizzie the Lizard goes on show at the Natural History Museum in London. She was found in Scotland, is 20cm long and is the oldest fossil reptile in the world.
Friday *November 18*	Happy birthday to Mickey Mouse! He made his debut in the first talkie cartoon *Steamboat Willie*, 60 years ago.
Saturday *November 19*	Prongy, the Bewick's Swan, arrives back from the Arctic at the Wildlife Trust, Slimbridge, Gloucs, for her 23rd winter with her mate Porcupine.
Sunday *November 20*	Allan Saldanha (11), from the City of London School, wins the Junior Scrabble Championship in South Kensington.

Snow closes roads in Scotland and the Pennines

Monday *November 21*	An RAF Vulcan bomber Dinky Toy is sold for £1250 at an auction of rare toys in Lewes, Sussex. European Space Agency's new *Ariane 4* rocket is rolled out to the launch pad in Kourou, French Guiana, for its launch next month when it will put the Astra TV satellite into orbit.
Tuesday *November 22*	The Queen rides to Westminster in her new ceremonial carriage with electric windows for the State Opening of Parliament. The new US B2 Stealth bomber makes its debut in California. It is made of special radar absorbent material so that it can slip undetected through enemy defences.
Wednesday *November 23*	Grand sumo champion Chionofuji, known as the Wolf, becomes only the fifth sumo wrestler in history to win 50 matches in a row.

Full Moon

Thursday *November 24*	Police close 4 London bridges as 20,000 students march in protest against student loan proposals. A new Children's Bill is outlined by the Government.
Friday *November 25*	Markku Alen and Ilka Kivimaki win the RAC Lombard Rally in a Lancia Delta Integrale.

Freezing fog

Saturday *November 26*	Start of National Tree Week. The Soviet Union launches a new three-man mission to the orbiting space station *Mir*, including Jean-Loup Chrétien of France.

Sunday *November 27*	John McCarthy, the British journalist who was kidnapped 2½yrs ago in Beirut, is 32 today.
Monday *November 28*	The Prime Minister, Mrs Thatcher, plants a birch tree in the Chelsea Physic Garden, London. A painting called *Acrobat and Young Harlequin* by Pablo Picasso is sold for £20,900,000 in London.
Tuesday *November 29*	French potholer Veronique Le Guen resurfaces after spending a record 110 days 76.2m underground in a cave in the Causses mountains.
Wednesday *November 30*	St Andrew's Day. Chia-Chia, the Giant Panda from London Zoo, is officially welcomed to Mexico City Zoo after a 3 month stay in Cincinnati. He moves in next door to his new mate Tohui.

Champions of 1988

Miss Pears	Sarah Cowie
Bisto Kids	Alexander and Lorelei Harwood
Boots Baby of the Year	Leanne Beaver
National Scrabble Champion	Margaret Rogers
Junior Scrabble Champion	Allan Saldanha
Toymaker of the Year	Tony Mann
Toy of the Year	Sylvanian Family
Crufts Supreme Champion	Starlite Express of Valsett
British Marbles Champions	Black Dog Boozers
London Taxi Driver of the Year	Paul Woodruff
Space Endurance Champions	Vladimir Titov and Musa Manarov
Boss of the Year	Anne Hawkins
Top Tea Place of the Year	Periwinkle Cottage Tearooms, Porlock
World Elver Eating Champion	Mark Ryder
FA Cup Champions	Wimbledon
European Soccer Champions	The Netherlands
International Worm Charming Champion	Nigel Canham
World Conker Champion	Will Cox
World Monopoly Champion	Ikuo Hiyakuta
Museum of the Year	The National Museum of Photography, Film and Television, Bradford
National Librarian of the Year	Sue Broughton
World Snail Champion	Tracker
The Times Crossword Champion	William Pilkington
Pig of the Year	Fenberry Catalina
Trans-Atlantic Yacht Champion	Philippe Poupon
National Backgammon Champion	James Moore
Wimbledon Women's Champion	Steffi Graf
Wimbledon Men's Champion	Stefan Edberg
Non-stop Singing Champion	Tiny Tim

December

Thursday *December 1*	World AIDS Day. An 18.29m high Christmas tree is lit at a ceremony at Mill Wall Dock, East London.
Friday *December 2*	Plymouth Health Authority bans fresh eggs from 25 hospitals in Devon after 78 cases of food poisoning. The US space shuttle *Atlantis* takes off from Cape Canaveral, with a 5-man crew, after a 24hr delay because of bad weather.
Saturday *December 3*	Lord Avebury plants an oak tree at Haywards Heath, Sussex, to commemorate the 40th anniversary of the signing of the United Nations Universal Declaration of Human Rights.
Sunday *December 4*	Seven new oak trees are planted at Sevenoaks, Kent, to replace the trees destroyed in last year's hurricane.
Monday *December 5*	Health Secretary, Kenneth Clarke, advises people to stop eating raw eggs because of the salmonella scare.
Tuesday *December 6*	Sergei Baltacha, of Dynamo Kiev, becomes the first Soviet soccer player to be signed up by an English club—Ipswich. 11-month-old heifer, Ebony (444kg), wins the Supreme Championship title at the Royal Smithfield Show, Earl's Court.
Wednesday *December 7*	The Cutting of the Chelsea Pensioners' Cheese in the Great Hall of the Royal Hospital, London. Every year since 1692, the great cheese has been distributed to the Chelsea Pensioners.
Thursday *December 8*	The Christmas tree in Trafalgar Square, London, is lit at 6pm. An earth tremor shakes Norwich, King's Lynn and Cromer, East Anglia.
Friday *December 9*	The DSS and the City of Edinburgh District Council win special Golden Bulls for gobbledygook at the Awards Ceremony of the Plain English Campaign in London. New Moon
Saturday *December 10*	2000 competitors take part in the National Cat Show, which opens at Olympia, West London, today.
Sunday *December 11*	The European Space Agency's *Ariane 4* rocket takes off from Kourou, French Guiana, with the new Astra TV satellite on board.
Monday *December 12*	Jean-Loup Chrétien takes the first French steps in space when he goes for a walk outside the orbiting Soviet space station *Mir*.
Tuesday *December 13*	The Old Curiosity Shop in Holborn, London, is for sale at £350,000. It was built in 1567 and is the oldest shop in London.

December

This used to be the tenth month in the old Roman Calendar when the year started in March.

Wednesday December 14
Fyona Campbell (21), from Scotland, arrives at Fremantle after walking 5,632.55km across Australia from Sydney in 95 days.

Thursday December 15
40 red double-decker buses sail for Sri Lanka from Sheerness, Essex.

Friday December 16
Junior Health Minister, Edwina Curry, resigns from the Government after egg sales plummet. Laurel and Hardy's bowler hats fail to reach their reserve price at a Christie's sale in London.

Saturday December 17
The Post newspaper, which was launched on Nov. 10, closes down after only 33 editions. 'Musicians for Armenia' concert at the Barbican, London, raises more than £1,000,000 for the Armenian Earthquake Appeal.

Sunday December 18
Max, a mongrel from Kippax, W. Yorks, is awarded the Pro Dogs medal for life-saving, and James, a corgi from Haverfordwest, is named Pet of the Year.

Monday December 19
A new environmental pressure group called Ark is born today. The repaired and regilded golden orb is placed back on top of the Central Tower spire at the Palace of Westminster.

Tuesday December 20
Princess Beatrice Elizabeth Mary of York is baptised with water from the River Jordan in the Chapel Royal, St James's Palace, wearing a christening robe made of Honiton lace.

NATIONAL TREE WEEK
(November 26–December 4)

National Tree Week is especially important because of the huge number of trees which were destroyed by the Great Hurricane of October 1987. Altogether, more than 600,000 trees are planted during National Tree Week.

2500 trees are planted in one hour near Birmingham at the start of the RSPB's Centenary Plantation. School children and professional footballers plant out the figure 1,000,000 in trees on a Yorkshire hillside. Acorn Kits are given to children in Derbyshire and an oak tree is planted in the middle of Mansfield, Nottinghamshire, to replace an ancient oak that used to be known as the middle of Sherwood Forest. In Kinlochmoidart seven saplings are planted as future replacements for a row of aged beech trees which commemorate the Seven Men of Moidart who accompanied Bonnie Prince Charlie to Glenfinnan.

Wednesday *December 21*	Soviet-French crew touch down in Central Asia from the orbiting space station *Mir*. Vladimir Titov and Musa Manarov have spent 365 days, 22hrs and 39mins in orbit, breaking the space endurance record set by Yuri Romanenko last year.
Thursday *December 22*	1.5 billion cards and letters are posted this Christmas—as well as 60,000,000 parcels. The Royal Mail uses helicopters and a hovercraft to make sure that everything is delivered on time.
Friday *December 23*	A box of mince pies is blown up by Army explosives experts in Oxford. The Isle of Skye ferry loses power in Force 11 gales and has to be rescued by a Royal Navy ship from Kyle. Full Moon
Saturday *December 24*	Christmas Eve. The Royal Family spend their Christmas holiday at Sandringham, Norfolk, for the first time in 25yrs because Windsor Castle is being repaired.
Sunday *December 25*	Christmas Day. It's so mild in London (12°C) that swimmers in the annual race on the Serpentine, Hyde Park, don't need a layer of grease to keep them warm—and sealions at the Regent's Park Zoo have lost their appetite.
Monday *December 26*	Boxing Day. A rare American robin, blown across the Atlantic by westerly gales, is spotted hopping around Inverbervie, Grampian. It's almost twice as big as a European robin.
Tuesday *December 27*	Circus animals are blessed at a special service held in the Big Top of Gerry Cottle and Austen's Circus in Battersea Park, London.
Wednesday *December 28*	The Volcano Lonquinay, which erupted in Chile, South America, for the first time in 100yrs on Boxing Day, sends gas, stones and ash 7,315.2m into the air.
Thursday *December 29*	Thousands of greedy Brent Geese, back from the Arctic for the winter, are ruining crops round Chichester Harbour, Sussex, and Langstone Harbour, Hants.
Friday *December 30*	A mystery 8km oil slick slithers ashore on the South Coast between Brighton and Bexhill. More than 100 sea birds, including guillemots and razorbills, are rescued and taken to the RSPCA Centre near Taunton.
Saturday *December 31*	New Year's Eve. 1000 runners take part in Nos Galen (Night of the New Year) torchlight race 6000m round the streets of Mountain Ash, Mid Glamorgan. It's held every year in memory of Guto Nyth Bran 'the fastest runner in the world', who died in 1737.